R

P9-CJZ-169

Magnolia Library

PRAISE

I really like the analogies throughout the chapters. They are outstanding for middle and high school students!

- Kurt, School Educator

My students are really enjoying it and we will be ordering more for the fall!

- Rebecca, School Educator

As a homeschooling mom, I really liked the handful of review questions the author added at the end of each chapter.

- Lisa, Homeschool Educator

First book I have read that covers everything we do in class! I am a big fan, easy to read and packed with good material.

- Dan, School Educator

Very easy to read! Small and portable, I like that I can carry it around anywhere. I learned a lot thanks to this book. Pizza, mmm.

- Felipe, Teenager

The teenage grandchildren that I bought these copies for said they really got a lot of insight from the book! They had their first experience with summer jobs and said this book helped them a great deal.

- Alden, Grandparent

This is the perfect supplemental reading for students in my financial management classes!

- Kristy, School Educator

PRAISE

The book is wonderfully well written, with a lighthearted and approachable style. It is just the thing for introducing young adults to the complexity of personal finance.

    - Dave, Parent

Easy and informative read. Great gift for graduates.

    - Cynthia, Parent

I love the concept and the way it is written. It is exactly what I needed for my son!

    - Brandi, Homeschool Educator

You have captured everything I teach into a 60-page book!

    - Joe, School Educator

This is the first book I have read that addresses everyday personal money concerns about saving, investing and debt without giving a responsibility lecture or promising the fantasy that a get-rich how-to book indulges in.

    - Anonymous, Parent

Our family is all in on I Want More Pizza. I have passed along our excitement for the program to the other families in our group!

    - Karen, Homeschool Educator

I read your book this morning and love it for my clients. Already gave one out at a meeting this morning and it was well received and appreciated.

    - Dave, Financial Planner

PERSONAL FINANCE

I WANT MORE

PIZZA

REAL WORLD MONEY SKILLS FOR
HIGH SCHOOL, COLLEGE, AND BEYOND

STEVE BURKHOLDER

Copyright © 2017 Overcome Publishing LLC
www.overcomepublishing.com

Volume discounts and customization of this book are available. Please email us at **steve@overcomepublishing.com** with any questions you may have. Also visit our Facebook page: *I Want More Pizza* Book.

All rights reserved. No portion of this book may be reproduced or transmitted in any form or by any means, electronic or manual—except for brief quotations in critical reviews or articles—without the prior written permission of the publisher.

This book is sold with the understanding that the publisher is not engaged in rendering financial, accounting, legal, or other professional services. Each individual situation is unique and, therefore, the publisher assumes no responsibility for financial success or failure. If financial advice or other expert assistance is required, the services of a competent professional should be sought.

Printed in the United States of America

Editorial: Rebecca Maizel and David Aretha, Yellow Bird Editors
Creative: McLeod, Dalipi, and Freepik

ISBN: 978-0-9965194-0-3
eBook ISBN: 978-0-9965194-1-0

It took about 65 people to make this book what it is today: 20 family and friends, 15 finance professionals, 5 publishing professionals, and 25 high school teachers and students. I would like to take this opportunity to thank each and every one of them. I am sure each reader (you) will become a *co-author* of this book in some way over time with your feedback. I want to thank you in advance.

I would like to dedicate
this book to

you.

Reading this book,
applying it in your life,
and passing your learning
along to others is truly
courageous.

CONTENTS

PREFACE

NEVER TOO YOUNG

When I was a young adult, personal finance was not always top of mind. I was busy worrying about who I was and who I wanted to be. I wondered, "Do I fit in?" "Am I doing well enough in school for my parents to be proud of me?" "Am I doing well enough in sports?" I didn't have time to worry about personal finance.

I wish I knew then what I know now.

I was lucky; my parents knew about personal finance. They didn't buy me everything I wanted, nor could they. I had to save my own money for things like sports equipment or clothes my parents could not afford. Some of my friends had it easier. Their parents bought them everything they wanted. This frustrated me then, but I'm happy now because I learned important money lessons.

I wish I knew then what I know now

Even before I was a teen, my parents had me open a savings account at the local bank and called it my *Christmas* account. "This is a way to make sure you have enough money to buy Christmas presents," my mom said. I didn't know it at the time, but the account was really for a much bigger reason.

When I started working, my parents made me put at least half of everything I earned into the account. Having that account taught me how to save and what it took to buy things for myself and for others. It forced me to make decisions with my money and face the subsequent consequences. To be honest, I didn't really miss the things I had to give up in order to save. It just became a habit and it was fun to watch my savings grow. By mowing lawns, working at McDonald's, and saving half of everything I earned, I saved more than $5,000 in the Christmas account by the end of high school. Doing this on my own felt great, and my guess is it made my family feel great too.

By working hard in school and at my part-time jobs I was able to go to college. The first few years of college went well and I was on my way toward getting a good job, but I was always looking for ways to earn more money. One day in my junior year in college, I heard about the *stock market*. It sure seemed easy enough to me. I just invest my money in a company and, I figured, after a little while it gives me back more money than I had when I started. Easy money. I liked the sound of that.

But I didn't know enough about the stock market. My parents didn't use the stock market much; this wasn't a topic we discussed. I thought I could do it on my own. Unfortunately, I invested in very risky companies, and after a few months I had lost all of my money. My entire $5,000 in savings that took me many years to save was gone, and it was  never coming back. I didn't know the *risks* of the stock market and that got me into trouble.

Personal finance difficulties can come in many forms. For me it was losing my money in the stock market. For others it can be credit card, student loan, or other debt they did not know enough about before they agreed to it. If you or a family member has lost their job, or are working two jobs and still don't have enough money, debt can feel like your only option at times. Or, it can be as simple as having financial struggles later in life because of not understanding how important it is to start saving as soon as possible no matter how much money you have. These difficulties can also come in many levels of intensity. I had a $5,000 problem. For others it can be much, much more and can impact them their entire lives starting as a young adult.

Since college I have spent most of my life learning and applying finance concepts. Still, today I see too many people, young and old, making mistakes similar to the $5,000 mistake I made every day, including those close to me. I sincerely hope this book empowers you to take control of your financial future, for yourself and for those around you.

INTRODUCTION

"The number one problem in today's generation and economy is the lack of financial literacy."

—ALAN GREENSPAN

WHY ARE YOU READING THIS BOOK?

Maybe someone important in your life suggested you should learn more about personal finance. Possibly you want to learn how to have more money for yourself or maybe you are just thinking to yourself, "I am making money—what should I do with it?" Or perhaps you want to learn how to have more money to help support your family, friends, church, or community. Those are all great reasons to be reading this book. When I was your age I had the same questions as you about money. I have spent many years gaining financial knowledge and experience and am eager to share it with you. I am going to do everything I can to help you achieve your goals—because you can.

I used to believe getting a job and working hard was enough. Don't get me wrong, having a good-paying job is the best start you can have toward personal finance success—I encourage you to work hard to get that dream job. But, I have since learned getting the job and receiving a paycheck is only the start and there are many more decisions to be made with respect to money if you want to achieve your goals.

You are starting to earn more money. The allowances, money you earned from babysitting and mowing lawns, and the paycheck from your part-time job are really adding up. Now you want to go spend your money to reward yourself for working hard. Rewarding yourself is important, but what if you didn't spend *all* of it? Doing something small today, such as saving a small amount, can help you achieve something much larger in the future.

Say you saved $25 each month. That's $300 each year, and after three years you would have almost $1,000. That sure would be nice to have if you were saving for a car or college. What if you saved for more than a few years, perhaps a lifetime, and each year that number grew and grew and...? (Don't worry, not everything in this book will only help you a long time from now. Much of it helps you today.) If you saved $25 a month for the next 40 years, you would have saved $12,000 ($25 × 12 months × 40 years). Now we are getting somewhere.

Let me ask you a question: If you saved $12,000 of your money over 40 years, how much will you have saved? No, that's not a trick question. You may have expected the answer to be $12,000, but with personal finance tools you can have *more*, a lot more. After using these **You can turn $12k into $50k**

tools, you may have turned that $12,000 into $50,000. That's $38,000 ($50,000 – $12,000) of free money! This particular tool is related to a concept called *compound growth* and is discussed in the 3rd Slice of this book.

If you're working part-time right now during school, $25 a month may be a lot of money, so start with $5, or $10, or whatever you can save, even $1. Or, if you can, save more than $25. As long as you're saving something is what's important.

Personal finance is a set of tools to make it *easier* for you to keep your hard-earned money and to make it grow as quickly as possible. In turn, you can feel more confident your goals are going to be met throughout your life.

You may have heard of some of the concepts in this book. For example, a big part of this book is on *saving*. You probably know *what* saving is. But, are you actually saving? Are you saving enough? Whether it is a concept you have already heard of or not, this book will help you understand *why* you should apply it in your life and, of equal importance, *how* you will apply it in the real world.

And if you don't love math or finance, no problem. There are personal finance concepts for you as well. Same goes if you like to plan, or if you prefer to be spontaneous, and anywhere in between. If you like concepts that don't take up too much of your time, the *Auto-Saver* concept in the 2nd Slice is definitely for you. Those of us who realize a small change in our money habits today can make an enormous difference are the ones who are able sit back, relax, and enjoy the pizza in life.

Unfortunately, for many, this is not easy to do.

MENTAL BLOCKS

Think about something you know is really important to do, but you just can't get yourself to do at times. We all have something like this in our lives. Homework, work, or exercising are examples for many people. My excuse usually is **"I don't have time; I'll do it later."** But, when we think about how important it is to do our homework, to go to work and to exercise, and when they become habits, they all become easier. It's the same with personal finance.

We are all well aware money is important. In fact, it's so important it is the number one source of stress in America. About 70% of Americans have stress related to money, according to the American Psychological Association. That's 7 out every 10 people, which means that there is a good chance that you, one or more of your family members, or friends has money-related stress. You may be experiencing money-related stress already if you are helping your family pay for things or just to keep up with your social life. If it is not a source of stress for you right now, it likely will be at some point, unfortunately. Losing my $5,000 was very stressful, that's for sure. I never thought it would happen to me.

70% have STRESS related to money

Even with all of that stress and desire to be better with our money, a study by Northwestern Mutual revealed that approximately 60% of Americans say their personal finances need improvement. With a population of approximately 320 million in the United States, that's almost 200 million people who need help! Well, similar to homework, work,

60% SAY THEIR PERSONAL FINANCES NEED improvement

and exercising, many of us have a mental block impeding our success in personal finance. Here are some common mental blocks we have:

- "I'm young; I'll do it later."
- "I don't have enough time for it."
- "I don't make enough money for it."
- "I can't understand it."
- "I don't need it."

These mental blocks are just excuses all of us make at some point. I know I did. Through high school my mental block was a combination of **"I don't have enough time for it"** and **"I'm young; I'll do it later."** I knew I needed money to buy things and

I needed to save. But I didn't know I could make a mistake at a young age in the stock market that would impact me for years to come. I was not too young to learn about the stock market and I should have made time for it.

Given the amount of money they have made in their professions, celebrities could have the mental block of **"I don't need it."** Here is what a few of them said in relation to their finance habits:

> ❝ You can't take your lifestyle for granted. I've got tons of money, but I'm afraid to spend it. Knowing I don't even have a high school diploma to fall back on, I'm going to be really careful with what I've got. ❞
>
> —*DAVE GROHL*

> ❝ Why do people look at me like I'm crazy when I use coupons at grocery (stores) or try bargaining at retail? I'm from New York. Where is the sale rack? ❞
>
> —*LADY GAGA*

> ❝ I don't spend money on a lot. Money is very important to me because it allows me the freedom to choose what I want to do as an actor and most importantly because I want to accumulate enough so that one day I can do something really great and beneficial for other people, for the environment or for children. ❞
>
> —*LEONARDO DICAPRIO*

> ❝ I am frugal. I've always been this way. When I was young, my mom would give me my allowance, and I'd peel off a little each week and have some to spare. ❞
>
> —*TYRA BANKS*

In some shape or form everyone needs to understand and apply personal finance. In my opinion, all of these celebrities have done a great job overcoming their mental block.

❺ Think about and determine your mental block. Keep it in mind as you read this book to help you overcome. This will be the most important thing you do if you want to be successful in personal finance.

MOVING FORWARD

Mental blocks can be amplified when we become overwhelmed. This is definitely the case for me. Personal finance has many, many facets: saving, compound growth, investing, debt, taxes, retirement, inflation, insurance, identify theft, and the list goes on. Overwhelmed yet?

Remember back many years ago when you first learned how to write. Did you write an entire paragraph? My guess is you probably started with a single letter. And with math, did you start with multiplication? That would have been a bit overwhelming.

This book focuses on the foundation of personal finance, which is everything you need right now. Here is the simple philosophy I recommend for you at this stage of your life:

- Overcome your mental block
- Save
- Don't get into trouble with debt or investing

By accomplishing this you can be successful at personal finance, and I will give you different options throughout the book as to how to do this in the real world. You have already started overcoming your mental block. Let's get started on the other areas, starting with saving.

Saving is the foundational crust of your personal finance pizza, $1 at a time. Everything leads back to saving in some way. For example, people invest to increase their *savings*. They protect their identities to make sure someone doesn't steal their *savings*. And people buy insurance to protect their *savings*. Without *savings*, you would not have any money to invest and you would not have any money to protect. As you can see, without *savings*, many of the more complicated aspects of personal finance are less relevant. Saving is the essential first step toward success.

70%

DON'T HAVE ENOUGH
SAVINGS FOR
UNEXPECTED EXPENSES

According to a Bankrate study, however, about 70% of Americans are living paycheck to paycheck, spending their entire paycheck by the time they get their next paycheck, and as a result don't have enough *savings* for unexpected expenses. About 70% of Americans have stress related to money, 60% of Americans say their personal finance needs improvement, and 70% of Americans don't have enough savings for unexpected expenses. I don't believe the similar magnitude of these statistics is a coincidence—saving is the solution.

Unexpected expenses, such as paying to get your car fixed, will happen to you. They happen to everyone. I can definitely see how it would be stressful for those who didn't manage their money well enough to have enough savings. Unfortunately, most people don't even get past their mental block to give saving a try, but you will in the 2nd Slice. When you do, you will already be more successful with personal finance than the 70% of Americans who don't.

In the 4th Slice we'll add some cheese to our pizza: debt. After you master the art of saving, the worst that could happen is you lose it. A very common way people lose their savings, or inhibit their ability to save in the first place, is by having excess debt such as credit card and student loan debt.

According to the Jump$tart Coalition for Personal Financial Literacy, about 30% of high school seniors use credit cards, and Nellie Mae states, on average, they have $1,600 of credit card debt. It takes a long time to save $1,600 as a young adult. Credit card companies spend hundreds of millions of dollars each year on advertising directed at teens; it is easy to understand why this happens.

HIGH SCHOOL SENIORS WHO USE CREDIT CARDS HAVE ABOUT

$1,600 in debt

The statistics for adults are even worse, much worse. Just like saving $1 at a time can lead to significant savings, unfortunately credit card debt $1 at a time can lead to significant debt. For most it starts off with a few small purchases such as a new pair of athletic shoes or a couple of lunches at your favorite burger restaurant. They promise themselves to pay off the credit card bill in full and on time, but they don't. Research by the Financial Industry Regulatory Authority showed about 60% of people with credit cards do not pay off their credit card bill in full and on time, carry a balance, and pay interest. There is that percentage again, showing you the importance of savings.

Wait; don't forget the sauce for your finance pizza! I call it *growing your savings*, which is comprised of investing and compound growth, which is the earlier concept that turned $12,000 into $50,000. This is covered in the 3rd Slice. The reason I have included investing is probably already clear as it is near and dear to my heart as another significant way to lose your savings. On the positive side, however, as long as you understand the risks better than I did at your age, investing and compound growth can be the best way to grow your savings. The previous example that turns $12,000 into $50,000 using compound growth is real, very real. Some say they can't afford to save right now or **"I don't make enough money for it,"** but I would argue due to compound growth they can't afford *not* to save.

It is entirely possible to live similar to how you live today *and* save at the same time. How different will your life be if you start spending $10 less each month on your phone? Sure, it would have a little impact, but not much. Yet, that little impact today can have a gigantic positive outcome for your future, just like that $25 each month turning into $50,000 one day.

You can live similar AND *save*

Also, I understand everyone is different. Some people enjoy eating pizza every day, while others like it every once in a while. Some people prefer a nice, simple cheese pizza; others like it with every topping possible. It's pepperoni, mushroom, and onion for me these days. But, most of us started with a cheese pizza and went from there. It's the same with personal finance and applying it into your real life. I do not believe there is a *right* or *wrong* answer with respect to personal finance. Rather, the right answer is the personal finance plan that works for *you* and only you. No one cares about your money as much as you do. No one.

You will find it feels great to be financially independent.

This book will provide you with a ton of real world examples to help you learn these foundational concepts. I will provide you with options you can choose from to overcome your mental block and put your personal learning into action in your life starting today (each item is marked with a ❸ throughout the book and then summarized at the end of the book in The End section). If you have any questions along the way, please feel free to contact me at my Facebook page (*I Want More Pizza Book*).

Here we go. After all, there's more pizza in life to be enjoyed.

It will feel *great* to be financially *independent!*

1st SLICE: YOU

YOUR ADVANTAGE

You have an advantage with personal finance over most people. You absolutely do because you are young and have *time* on your side.

For many personal finance concepts, time is what makes them work best. It is important to have knowledge and a good-paying job, but without time it is more difficult to be successful. For example, do you think it would be easier to save $365 in one day or, rather, by saving $1 each day for a year? I have a lot of knowledge, but I can't make $365 magically appear overnight; it takes time, which you have.

This is one example of how time helps you save. You will really see the importance of time with the compound growth concept in the 3rd Slice. This concept will show you how to earn free money over time. The more time you have, the more free money you will acquire. As you are reading, the importance of time will become more and more evident to you. With that in mind, let's start taking action!

YOUR ACTION

What do you believe is the most important thing to do next on your path toward personal finance success? The answer: Something. Anything.

Many people research how to exercise for hours and hours at home so they have the *perfect* workout, but then never actually go to the gym. My guess is you burn more calories doing even the *wrong* workout compared to not going to the gym at all. Once you are in the habit of going to the gym you can perfect the workout, but that initial action of going is the key to success. It's the same with personal finance. No matter how much you know about personal finance, none of that will matter until you take action and do something about it. I can't emphasize this enough.

If you are afraid of making a mistake, that is natural. Many of us learn from making our own mistakes or from others' mistakes. In fact, everyone makes mistakes with personal finance. I did and you will too. So, if you are worried, you might as well make that mistake now and start learning from it. It can be much easier to recover from a mistake early in life compared to when you are older.

only
14%
OF TEENS SAY HAVE
TAKEN A CLASS ON
financial literacy

Capital One research shows that only 14% of teens have acted and taken a class on a financial literacy topic. The fact you're reading this book means you're already a lot closer than many to taking control over your money because you're aware of the importance of personal finance—something needs to be done and you're actually doing it.

YOUR GOALS

Understanding what your goals are and the role money plays in achieving them will help you overcome your mental block and take action. After all, the reason you are learning more about personal finance is to make sure you can achieve your goals.

For many, the first thing that comes to mind when they hear personal finance is having more money. This is true and for some that is enough. Money itself was not enough to motivate me to be successful. The comfort the money was going to provide my life was my motivation. Since I was not worried about money as much after I had succeeded with personal finance, I could focus on the people I love, my health, and the things I enjoy doing.

What are *your* dreams in life? Those are your goals.

They can be small goals such as buying a ticket to that music concert you've been waiting to go to, or larger goals such as buying your first car. They can be shorter-term goals for the near future like saving that $25 next month, or longer-term goals for

what are your
Dreams?

a long time from now such as your wedding. The average wedding costs $28,000!

Knowing and achieving these goals makes personal finance more enjoyable. It was always a dream of mine to travel to another country. I saved for a long time in order to go on a backpacking trip throughout Europe a few years after I graduated college. One of my stops was the Olympics in Greece. It was really easy to save when I thought about what it was for. The trip was worth every penny to me and was an experience I'll never forget.

⊗ Think about your goals and write them down. Have fun with this one; it's your chance to dream big. For this and all other exercises in this book I have created templates for you to fill in if you like. You can find them at **www.overcomepublishing.com/solution/**.

Perhaps you want to help your family financially, pay for college or a home, or become an entrepreneur. I bet you came up with great goals. Remember, they're *your* goals. Let's keep moving toward achieving your goals—it's exciting!

YOUR PRIORITIZATION

"If you can, you will quickly find that the greatest rate of return you will earn is on your own personal spending. Being a smart shopper is the first step to getting rich."

—*MARK CUBAN*

You may not have known it, but each financial decision you make involves two sides—the item you're buying and, of equal importance, the item you're giving up.

For example, you have $20 in your pocket and find a T-shirt you love at your favorite store in the mall and it costs $20. But, you also wanted to give that $20 to your family to help buy groceries. You choose the groceries and it feels great to help out. As a result, however, you gave up the T-shirt. You *prioritized* the groceries over the T-shirt.

Understanding that each financial decision you make involves two sides is as simple as it sounds, but oh so important. If you have the mental block of **"I don't make enough money for it,"** this will help you make better decisions with the money you do have. A small change today can have a significant impact over your lifetime. Let's take this concept one step further.

Say you like to drink a $5 coffee about twice a week or 10 times a month (or anything else you routinely spend money on—for me it's ice cream and, as you already know, pizza, but it doesn't have to be food; maybe it is phone apps or music for you). No problem, but what are you giving up?

Hint: It's not another $5 item.

At $5 per coffee, 10 times a month for 12 months, those coffees add up to $600 each year ($5 × 10 times × 12 months = $600)! So, in this instance, you gave up $600 worth of other stuff.

Coffee *vs.* new *tablet*

Maybe a new tablet was what you gave up this time as a result of the coffees. Or, over several years of coffee drinking, perhaps it was a car. If you knew this, would you still prioritize the coffee over the tablet or car? Maybe, maybe not.

It's YOUR *choice*

If you don't really need a new tablet or a car, it's your choice to drink coffee to your heart's content. Or, now that you know what you're giving up, perhaps you want to change your prioritization. Perhaps you cut down to five coffees a month and put the money you would have spent on the other five coffees away to save for that new tablet. That's a savings of $25 (5 coffees × $5) a month or almost $300 in a year; you'll have that tablet in no time. Or you could already be saving that $25 a month on your way to $50,000 and we are just getting started! Sometimes it's the *small stuff* that makes all the difference in meeting your goals. We'll take a closer look at this in the 2nd Slice in the *Sweat the Small Stuff* section.

sometimes *it's the* small stuff

Here is an example of prioritization:

The Current List is a list of items you may need to buy that is not prioritized. We all buy a lot of things; your real-life list may be different. If you only have $500, with the total of the Current List being $750, you will run out of money before you get to the end of this list. At the end of the list is college application fees and, if that is really important to you, it may be quite disappointing that you have run out of money.

CURRENT LIST	
Savings	$25
Clothes	100
Video Games	35
Food	50
Car	180
Music	60
Movies	55
Books	15
Phone	80
Coffee	25
College Applications	125
TOTAL	**$750**

PRIORITIZED LIST

IST PRIORITY		2ND PRIORITY		3RD PRIORITY	
Savings	$25	Car	$180	Music	$60
Clothes	100	Phone	80	Movies	55
College Applications	130			Video Games	35
Food	50			Coffee	25
				Books	15
SUBTOTAL	$300	SUBTOTAL	$260	SUBTOTAL	$190
				TOTAL	$750

The Prioritized List is the same list of items as in the Current List; however, you have them prioritized by importance. With the Prioritized List, you would start your spending at the 1st priority and work your way through the 2nd and 3rd priorities. With your $500, you have no problem paying for the college application fees, since the 1st Priority items in total only cost $300. As such, you have $200 ($500 – $300) left for the 2nd Priority items. Will you be able to buy all of the 2nd Priority items?

Unfortunately not.

Maybe you see this problem and decide you will use public transportation as opposed to buying a car so you can afford some books. Or perhaps all it takes is a less expensive car so you can have both and that works best for you. What is important is you see the problem before it is too late and adjust your spending accordingly.

When I first learned this concept, it made me feel like I was going to have to sit around saving while the fun things in life passed me by.

As I applied it to my real life, however, I realized this was not the case. Rather, spending less money on the things that *were not* important to me gave me a better chance at having everything that *was* important to me.

have enough *money* for what IS *important*

One thing I gave up was eating out at restaurants as much because that was not important to me. In return, in addition to saving more each month, I am able to take more trips. I love those travel experiences and the memories that will be with me forever. I would have to say that my favorite trip was an African safari in Tanzania. And when I am on vacation and spending money, I am not stressed out. Because I prioritized my spending and saved money, I am comfortable that I have the money to spend. It is nice to be able to have choices.

Feel free to add or delete items on the template that are not applicable to you and, in addition, change the dollar amounts for your specific circumstances. You can ask your family and friends to help you create this list as well, especially for expenses you don't have now but might have in the future such as rent. Or, maybe observe them spending money—for example at the grocery store or paying monthly bills. The list gets long and expensive quickly! You will see a lot of big numbers in this book that might surprise you. The numbers are real. Things we all love cost money, and that is the reality of it.

⑤ Think about what's important to you. How will you prioritize your spending to help achieve your goals?

So what is important to you? Perhaps shoes, vacations, or giving to your church or charity are your priorities. Of equal importance, what was *not* important to you and didn't make the list? Maybe going to music concerts became less of a priority, and by spending less on these it can help you save. Remember, this is *your* prioritization.

After a while, you won't even notice that the less important things are gone. What you will notice is in their place you'll have savings and more certainty with respect to your money and your future. How good would that feel? Ahhhhhh, to be financially independent.

YOU SUMMARY

You are your best friend when it comes to success at personal finance, but, unfortunately, you are also your worst enemy. For those who do not take action, money will probably always be a struggle. Now that you know your advantage of time and, further, your goals, and that you might need money to achieve them, use this as your motivation. Understanding and applying your prioritization is a good start. Let's continue taking action and moving closer to achieving those goals of yours.

REAL WORLD KNOWLEDGE SHARING

In addition to reading this book, I believe talking about personal finance with others will really help you as well. Hearing what they have learned, the success they have achieved, and, also importantly, the mistakes they have made in the real world will be extremely valuable. Share with your friends and family. In addition, my Facebook page (*I Want More Pizza* Book) serves as a 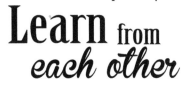 forum for everyone who reads this book to share their stories.

Feel free to talk about anything you want, of course, but to get you started I will have a few questions at the end of each Slice, like these:

- Do you have money-related stress?
- Why do you want to be successful with personal finance?
- Who that you know has attempted to learn (taken a class, read a book, etc.) about personal finance?
- What are the most expensive things you spend (or will spend) your money on?
- What does *prioritization* mean to you?

NOTES

NOTES

NOTES

2ND SLICE: SAVING

> **"Do not save what is left after spending, but spend what is left after saving. If you buy things you do not need, soon you will have to sell the things you need."**
>
> *—WARREN BUFFET*

Yes, you already know what *saving* is. You took a bunch of pictures on your phone and you're *saving* them to show to your friends later. Then you bought a pizza and *saved* half of it for later. It's the same with money—you're *saving* it for later for one reason or another.

Knowing *what* saving is the easy part. Knowing *why* you should save and *how* to do it is the tough part for many. Remember, about 70% of Americans don't have enough savings for unexpected expenses. I want you to have enough money to be comfortable, no matter what unexpected expenses come your way. Here are a couple of questions you may be asking yourself:

WHY SHOULD I SAVE?

As you know, personal finance takes motivation to be successful. We're all saving for a reason, and for most of us it all comes back to the same place—happiness, achieving our dreams, and supporting our values. The main reason I save is to make sure my family has everything they need, always, and that makes me happy. I want them to be proud of me. Why do *you* want to save? Perhaps the better question to ask yourself is: "How will saving help me achieve my goals?"

One reason people save is to buy more expensive items, such as nice clothes for an interview for your dream job, a new video gaming system, an education, or a home. You'll need to have savings to purchase these items.

Another reason people decide to save is because the future is unknown. Unexpected expenses will happen in your life. Sometimes they're for the good, such as your friends deciding last minute to go to a music concert and a ticket costs $100. But other times, unfortunate things happen, such as your car breaking down. This might cost you $500 to get it fixed. Ugh, not fun. If you're not saving, these surprises may be a big problem for you. Could you live without your car for a few months while you save up the $500? What if something worse happened? What if you or a family member lost their job? If you have savings, these financial surprises will have a much smaller impact on your life. You'll be at that music concert, stress free—well, except when you are deciding what to wear!

People also save to take advantage of the power of compound growth, which you will learn about in the 3rd Slice. This is the concept that turned your $12,000 into $50,000. You can use the compound growth tool for goals throughout your life—even retirement. While I know retirement is a long way away for you, it's important to think about today. Accumulating the amount of money you'll need for retirement takes time. In fact, for most, it takes a lifetime. Many people think they'll start later and catch up, but when the time comes they discover it's not possible to do so and they have to work later in life. I can't imagine how stressful it would be to learn at a later age that I didn't have enough and could not retire, and don't ever want to know. In fact, according to a Gallup poll, the average retirement age in America is quickly approaching 70. On my goals list, I have a retirement age of much younger than 70. The earlier you start saving, the earlier you may be able to retire. It's as simple as that.

And to be honest, saving just feels good for many people. Have you ever gone shopping and got a really good deal on something? You went to the store to buy that pair of shoes you have been waiting months to wear and show your friends and they were 25% off! I love that feeling. That is how saving makes me feel.

WHAT IF I DON'T HAVE A LOT OF MONEY?

You may be working part-time or have just started working and are making minimum wage. Maybe one of your parents cannot work due to health reasons, or you only have one parent, or perhaps you don't have any parents and you have to help with the household expenses.

Some people have money; some are hoping to have enough money to have food for the week. I hope that I can show you everyone has enough money to save a certain amount toward personal finance success.

Just remember that $1 saved is better than $0, every time, so take it $1 at a time. The highest wage I had in high school was $5.70 an hour, just above minimum wage. Everyone has to start somewhere, and higher wages will hopefully come over your lifetime. In addition to higher wages, decreasing your spending is another way to have more money. If one person earns $5,000 in a year and spends $4,000 of it and another person earns $100,000 in a year and spends all $100,000, who has more savings? Yes, the person who earned $5,000. How much you spend is equally important as how much money you earn. And, while higher wages are not always fully in your control, how much you spend is. You can change how much you spend today.

If you or your family does not have a lot of money right now, saving increases the likelihood of having financial success. The two concepts that worked best for me to save in high school were *Prioritization*, discussed in the 1st Slice, and the *Auto-Saver*, later in this Slice. Having money for those more expensive items, for unexpected expenses, and to take advantage of compound growth can reduce your stress today and increase your money in the future. At first, yes, saving will be difficult. You will have to live without certain things for a period of time, prioritizing only the necessities. But, after a while, when it becomes a habit, you will see your savings grow and it will become easier—especially when you start achieving your goals.

You can't afford *not* to save.

HOW DO I SAVE?

Personal finance is a set of tools to make it *easier* for you to keep your hard-earned money and to make it grow as quickly as possible. The best way I know *how* to save I call the *Auto-Saver*. Automatic savings—it doesn't get any easier than that.

THE AUTO-SAVER

Spoiler Alert: This is my favorite concept of the book (and compound growth)! If you are the type who does not like to plan, this topic is perfect—I have a trick for you. The trick is to trick yourself.

I bet you do this one way or another already. Maybe you want to exercise for an hour, but mentally this is challenging. If you're like me, you look at your watch every five minutes. Still 45 minutes left!?!? What makes it easier? Setting smaller goals is one possible answer. For example, you take a small break every 15 minutes, and then you only have to be mentally strong for 15 minutes as opposed to an entire hour; but in the end, you still get the full hour of exercise.

For school, perhaps you use a similar concept each day, focusing on when the next class will be done as opposed to looking all the way to the end of the day. And have you ever found $5 in your pocket you'd totally forgotten? What a surprise! Even if  you didn't find the money, you would've been just as happy. But when you find it, it's great.

The *Auto-Saver* is based on similar concepts. You'll hide the money from yourself before you get a chance to spend it. If it's out of sight, you won't spend it and, surprisingly enough, you won't even notice. I do this myself, as do many, many other successful savers. You're just two steps away…

Step One: Create Two Bank Accounts

There are a variety of bank account types, but two common types are *savings* and *checking* accounts. A savings account is just that, an account you save money in. Since you are saving money, this is an account you do not withdraw money from often. Rather, a checking account is an account you withdraw from more frequently for day-to-day expenses such as food.

For the *Auto-Saver*, you first create two bank accounts. The bank accounts can be with a large bank, such as a Wells Fargo or Citibank; banks that are only online, such as Capital One; or your smaller neighborhood bank or credit union—whichever you prefer. It can be a combination of a checking account and a savings account, two savings accounts, two checking accounts—whichever you prefer. My preference is one checking account and one savings account. Some banks try to charge you a fee for your bank accounts. There is no need to pay a fee, so avoid accounts with fees associated with them.

If you don't have two bank accounts, go get them. If you want to stop reading the book right now to go do this, I'll be here when you get back. Oh, and at most banks, you get to name your accounts, so have some fun. Perhaps *Have Fun Today* (checking account) and *Enjoy Tomorrow* (savings account). Yes, I know, you'll come up with something much cooler than that I'm sure.

Step Two: Establish Recurring Transfers

Okay, now you have two bank accounts (or will soon). Now you will make your savings *automatic*. You do that by asking the bank to automatically transfer a portion of your money from one bank account to the other on a recurring basis; for example, every month. You'll only need to ask the bank one time to set up this recurring transfer and they'll automatically do it every month until you tell them to stop. Here is how it will work.

Let's assume you asked the bank to automatically transfer $25 from your checking account to your savings account once a month. When you receive money, such as a paycheck or money you earn by babysitting, mowing lawns, other jobs, or your allowance—say $300 a month—you deposit it into the checking account. You're done, and now it is the bank's turn. The bank will then automatically transfer $25 every month to the savings account, like this:

YOU			BANK
PAYCHECK	⇨	**CHECKING ACCOUNT** ⇨	**SAVINGS ACCOUNT**
$300		**$300-$25 = $275**	**$25**

In this example, for this month you'll have $275 left in your checking account for your day-to-day purchases and $25 in your savings account to help you reach your goals.

All you have to do is deposit the money you receive in your checking account. And after you've done that? You guessed it. Nothing. You don't look at the savings account (or at least don't spend it, as it might be fun to look at). That way, you're *tricking* yourself into saving. The savings account will grow automatically: $25, $50, $75…$300 after a year. Instead of finding $5 in your pocket, you could *find* $300 in your *pocket*!

💲 Create two accounts at your bank and set up the automatic transfer to Auto-Save.

I know tricking yourself sounds pretty weird, but it works. This is essentially the way I saved my $5,000 in high school. The only difference is my automatic transfer was done by my parents forcing me to save—I didn't have another option, just like you won't after you

set up the recurring transfer with your bank, and that is a good thing.

If you have the mental block of **"I don't have enough time for it,"** I hope this concept shows you that saving doesn't need to take much time at all. You may be working two jobs, working while going to school, or helping your family with chores, not to mention your social calendar. Your time is important. The savings account grows automatically and your lifestyle won't skip a beat. You'll feel good knowing you're saving and, if an unexpected expense occurs, no problem, you've got it covered.

You *Auto-Saver* you!

WHERE DID ALL OF MY MONEY GO?

Well, now that you are an *Auto-Saver*, you already know where a portion, say $25 a month, of your money goes: savings. What about the rest?

You work hard, get paid, and are happy because once again all is well with money. Then, the next time a friend asks you to go to the movies, you check your wallet or purse and are disappointed. You ask yourself that dreaded question: "Where did all of my money go?" Most just promise to themselves they are going to spend less next month. But then next month comes and goes, and the next month, and the next, and they are still asking themselves this same question.

Think about something you want to do well at. Perhaps it is sports, video games, school, or the arts. If you aren't doing well, you probably don't just say "I'll do better next time" and stop there. No, you talk to your teacher or coach and learn what you are doing wrong and how you can get better. Put another way, you understand what happened last time and come up with a plan on how to do better next time. This is the same way you'll answer the question of "Where did all of my money go?"

If you don't know what happened *last* time with your money, it is really hard to make it better the *next* time. So, by making a list of where your money *actually* went last week or month, you will know exactly where you want to improve your spending habits.

Here's how you can do this. First, pick the time period to track your expenses. Maybe you keep track of where your money goes for the next week or the next month—whatever works for you. To create your list, you can use a spreadsheet program such as Excel or Google Sheets. I'm sure you're twice as good with computers than I was at your age (although I will admit I am an Excel nerd these days). If you do not have a computer or tablet with Excel, your school or local library may have one you can use.

Phones can be another way to create your list. You can use the spreadsheet program on your phone if that is available, or a notepad or similar type function. Or, if you prefer paper, maybe have a notebook that is specifically designated for your individual personal finance plan, including this list. Phones and notebooks can be good because you can have them with you and write down what you are spending right when you spend it. Or you can keep your receipts, bank statements, or credit or debit card statements and create your list from those documents later at home—whichever your preference. As long as you create it, that's what's important.

On the next page is a template to get you started making your list. All of the lines in the template may or may not be applicable to you, and feel free to add or remove lines.

⑤ Keep track of everything you spend next week or month using a spreadsheet or any other format that works best for you. Are any changes necessary to reach your goals? Prioritize, prioritize, prioritize.

Did anything on the list surprise you? That $600 a year you were spending on coffee in our earlier example in the 1st Slice would become very obvious. When it is $5 at a time, we just don't think about it much, but when this list adds them all up, it is hard to ignore. If you have the mental block of **"I don't make enough money for it,"** this will really help you understand every dollar you have and be able to do exactly what you want with those dollars.

And now the most important part: deciding if there is anything you should spend less money on to make sure you have

Did anything *surprise* you?

money for the important things, such as going to the movies with your friends. Prioritization will be an important tool for you. Perhaps you decide to spend less on your car so you can have more money for music concerts. Or maybe it's your clothes you want to spend less money on so you can make sure to save your $25 each month. Or is it both? It is your decision.

WHERE DID ALL OF MY MONEY GO?	
CATEGORY	AMOUNT
Saving	$ _____
Clothes	$ _____
Food	$ _____
Car	$ _____
Shoes	$ _____
Video Games	$ _____
Music	$ _____
Movies	$ _____
Books	$ _____
Phone	$ _____
Coffee	$ _____
College	$ _____
_____	$ _____
_____	$ _____
TOTAL	$ _____

I went through this exercise recently and my *entertainment* area was the one that surprised me. I discovered I spent a lot of money on music, going to the movies, and buying new books. I now listen to free online music, rent movies, and buy used books more than I did before. It is paying off and I am just as happy as before.

After you have done this once, you can decide if and when you would like to do it again. Some people do this every month or every year. For others the next time they do it is the next time they start asking themselves that ever important question: "Where did all of my money go?" And for others they never do it again as they just naturally become more conscious of their spending once they know where their money is going. The frequency that helps you achieve your goals is the right answer for you.

Still need help figuring out where to spend less? Sweating the small stuff might be just the help you need...

SWEAT THE SMALL STUFF

"Beware of little expenses; a small leak will sink a great ship."
—BENJAMIN FRANKLIN

How long does it take you to decide to buy something expensive, such as a new $300 tablet? Possibly a few days, or even longer. After all, it is a lot of money. How about a smaller, less expensive item such as a $5 coffee? Maybe only a few minutes. When you're spending a lot of money at one time like you are on the tablet, it's natural to think about your decision. The problem is, however, the $5 coffee is actually the larger financial decision to make.

Small stuff **Adds up!**

Having a $5 coffee 10 times each month costs you $600 ($5 × 10 times × 12 months = $600) each year, which is a lot more than the $300 tablet. I would think a lot about a $600 purchase. As a result, most people actually have trouble saving because of the small purchases adding up; for example, $5 at a time, as opposed to the individually large purchases they make. They just didn't know this, but now *you* do.

What if you could either have those coffees, or have half that amount of coffees, which will cost you $300 a year, *and* that new $300 tablet? It's the same amount of money, $600. As you can see, you're already given this choice every day. This is a great example of prioritization.

Neither choice is right or wrong. If you want more coffee, go for it. If you really want that tablet, then giving up a couple of coffees won't be a problem—have fun showing off that new tablet to your friends. Or, maybe you decide you don't want the tablet anymore and now have newfound savings!

❾ Make a list of all the *small stuff* in your life that you can live without if it meant helping you reach your goals.

When I go out to eat at a restaurant, I almost always get tap water to drink. That saves me about $3 every time. I don't miss the soda I used to drink all of the time—and my health is probably better for it. This type of habit has spread into other parts of my life as well and, although it may not seem like much, those $3 items really add up. If I have even one less soda each week, that's $156 a year saved ($3 per week × 52 weeks) just by drinking less soda! On the topic of water, I often have a water bottle with me so that I do not have to buy a bottle of water. Saving money and the environment!

For fun, I'll share another one with you—haircuts. Yes, I will admit it, I cut my own hair. It saves me about $20 a month or $240 a year ($20 per month × 12 months)! By using the compound growth concept in the 3rd Slice of this book, it will be much, much more over the years.

These could work for you as well, or perhaps you prefer to spend a little less on makeup or video games. Maybe it's clothes or your phone. Or possibly it's $5 less a month of all of these that helps you get to your savings goal in total. It's your call. What's important is you're aware that small purchases can add up to large dollar amounts over time. Remember, we're saving a lot of money $1 at a time.

SAVING SUMMARY

You now have a strong set of tools. By using the *Auto-Saver* concept, if you don't touch the money in the savings account, you are guaranteed to save. After a while, they become habits and you'll enjoy the

financial security. Challenge your friends and family—see how much you all can save while being as happy, or happier, than you were before. As long as you're saving, you're succeeding.

It's also important to occasionally reward yourself along the way. Buy yourself something, buy your family or friend a gift, or maybe give to someone you don't know—whatever makes you feel good. After all, you're saving for a reason—go achieve those goals!

REAL WORLD KNOWLEDGE SHARING

- If you didn't have any savings, what would you be most worried about?
- What are the two steps you need to take to become an *Auto-Saver?*
- What could you spend less on and not even notice it in your life?
- How much are you going to save?
- Can you afford *not* to save?

NOTES

NOTES

NOTES

3RD SLICE: GROWING YOUR SAVINGS

Now that you know how to save, you've started to take control of your financial future. I can't emphasize enough how important saving is as the foundation of personal finance—it's the crust of your pizza. Let's put on some sauce by learning how to grow your savings.

If you have the mental block of **"I'm young, I'll do it later,"** this Slice is definitely for you. The financial tools you will learn in this Slice work even better over time. If you don't start today, you lose out on savings you can never get back.

Of course, one sure way to grow your savings is to save more—so keep doing that. Similar to the *Auto-Saver*, this Slice shows you concepts that help you grow your savings almost automatically. This Slice shows you how to put the money you have already have to *work* for you. This probably sounds

Put your *money* to work for you!

really good if you have either the mental block of **"I don't make enough money for it"** or **"I don't have enough time for it."** "How do I put my money to work and grow my savings automatically," you may be thinking. I thought you'd never ask...

INVESTING

Investing is when you lend money to, or pay to acquire ownership in, another party such as a bank, the government, or a company, with the expectation that, after time, the other party will repay you *more* money than you originally provided them. First and foremost, it is important to understand there are risks to investing. I lost my $5,000 because I did not understand these risks. Now that I have learned about investing, I know the benefits far outweigh the risks. I really enjoy having my money *work* for me. After you have learned the risks, I encourage you to take advantage of the benefits.

THE BASICS

When people hear the word *investing*, many think about buying stocks in the stock market. That is only one of many types of investing. A savings account, just like the one you used to become an *Auto-Saver*, is another type of investment. Here are five common forms of investing:

SAVINGS ACCOUNT

This is the same savings account we discussed in the 2nd Slice of the book for the *Auto-Saver* tool. This is where you lend money to your bank and in return the bank pays you interest.

CERTIFICATE OF DEPOSIT

This is similar to a savings account. The primary difference is for a certificate of deposit (CD) you agree to lend your money to the bank for a fixed amount of time, such as a certain number of months or years. In return for this agreement, the bank pays you a higher interest rate than a savings account.

STOCKS

Companies have *stock* you can purchase. In return, you own a portion of the company. Also in return, you'll own a portion of the company's performance. In order to get your money back, you'll have to sell the stock you own to someone else. If the company you invested in has performed well since you purchased the stock, you may be able to sell the stock for a higher price than what you bought it for and earn money. However, if the company has performed poorly, you may have to sell the stock for a lower price than what you bought it for and, in turn, you'll *lose* money (more on the risk of losing money later in this section). You can invest in stocks in several different ways. You can buy stocks directly at some banks. Another option is purchasing stocks with online retail brokerages such as eTrade or Ameritrade. You can also choose an individual financial advisor close to your home to help you invest if you prefer to meet someone in person, such as Northwestern Mutual or TD Waterhouse. Whichever you are most comfortable with is the best answer. Buying and selling stocks is the easy part. Buying and selling stocks that make you money is the more difficult part. Even though I had a bad first experience with the stock market when I lost my $5,000, I still invest in the stock market today. I now know and appreciate the risk and enjoy the rewards.

There is an *investment* type that's right for *you*.

US TREASURY BONDS

A common example of a bond is a US Treasury bond. This is similar to a certificate of deposit in that you agree to lend your money for a fixed period of time. The primary difference is you're lending your money to the United States government as opposed to a bank. Over time, the government pays you a form of interest. You can invest in these bonds through some banks or at **www.savingsbonds.gov.**

MUTUAL FUNDS

A mutual fund is a professionally managed group of individual investments; for example, a group of stocks in several different companies, within a single investment *fund*. With a single stock (investment type on previous page), the performance of only that individual company determines whether you earn or lose money. In a mutual fund, as there are multiple companies, some companies within the fund can do poorly, but as long as more perform well than those that do poorly, you'll earn money as opposed to lose money. This is also known as *diversifying* your investment, which reduces your risk (more on this later in this section). You can invest in mutual funds the same ways you invest in stocks and, in addition, you can invest with mutual fund-specific online institutions such as T. Rowe Price, Vanguard, Fidelity, and Van Kampen. (There are generally fees associated with buying and selling mutual funds and stocks. Also, there can be a minimum amount you have to invest. And there can be age restrictions as well; however, you can generally overcome these restrictions if you have an adult help you invest. Review these fees, minimums, and age restrictions when choosing where you will invest. You can learn more at **finance.yahoo.com**, **www.fool.com**, or **www.mfea.com**).

DID YOU SAY MORE MONEY?

You may have a lingering question. "Why does the other party pay me back *more* money than I originally lent them?"

Great question.

Let's first use the savings account investment type to help answer this. As you know, you are going to put some of your money into your savings account at the bank. For doing this, the bank is going to give you back *more* money than you initially deposited. The extra money the bank is going to give you is called *interest*. Interest is money you can either *receive* or *pay*. We'll focus on interest *received* in this Slice and will get into *paying* interest in the 4th Slice.

Interest is free money the banks want to give you. Yes, really, they want to give you free money. Here is why the bank would do that:

You give $25 to the bank.
↓
The bank gives your $25 to *someone else* (a third party).
↓
The bank makes *someone else*
pay them back $30 ($5 in interest).
↓
The bank then gives you back $27.
The extra $2 is interest. *You are happy.*
↓
The bank profits $3 ($5 − $2). *The bank is happy.*

The bank is more than happy to give you this free money because they're still making money. In any event, if they're paying it, you should gladly be taking the free money. I take this free money, every day.

The amount of interest you earn from the bank is generally disclosed to you when you lend them money, usually stated as a percentage (%). This percentage is called an *interest rate*. This is generally the way your savings account, CDs, and bonds work. Let's go through a quick example.

Say that after a while of saving your $25 a month you have $1,000 in your savings account. Assuming a 1% annual interest rate, for example, you'll have $1,010 in a year's time because you'll have earned $10 of interest from the bank ($1,000 × 1%). The $10 truly is free money! We'll continue with this example in the compound growth section later in this Slice because $10 is just the start. Before we go further into the benefits, I want to finish our discussion on the risks of investing.

RISK VERSUS REWARD

WARNING: When investing, you can make money or lose money.

Let me say that again. It's possible to *lose* money when investing. This warning is only meant to ensure you're aware there's risk involved with

investing. Most people invest at some point in their life as the benefits outweigh the risks for them. It's just important to learn about it and understand what actions you're taking. This is another reason why it is important to overcome mental blocks such as **"I'm young; I'll do it later"** and **"I don't need it."** This section will show you that some investments have almost no risk of losing money, such as your savings account, CD and US Treasury Bonds, while others have a higher risk of losing money. Here's how it can work with investments with higher risk, such as mutual funds and stocks:

You give a portion of your money to another party.

⬇

The other party uses your money in an attempt to make more money for themselves.

⬇

The other party either performs well or poorly.

⬇

If the other party performs well, you may get back your money plus a portion of the other party's performance. *If* the other party performs poorly, you may share a portion of their loss, and they will give you back less than the amount of money you gave them originally.

Some things have lower levels of risk, while others have higher levels of risk. Walking across the street has a lower risk, while skydiving has a higher risk. It's similar in investing. Here are our five investment examples on a risk spectrum (as a general rule):

LOWER RISK			HIGHER RISK	
Savings Account ⇨	CDs ⇨	Treasury Bonds ⇨	Mutual Funds ⇨	Stocks

So why would people buy the higher-risk investments? Why not just buy the lower-risk investments? With the additional risk, you potentially receive a higher *reward*—with skydiving the reward is in the form of excitement. I went skydiving in Australia on one of my trips; excitement is an understatement! Of course, there's also the possibility of a potentially larger loss as well. This is the same with investments, except it's in the form of money.

The higher the risk, the potentially higher amount of money you could make or, unfortunately, lose. For example, one of the primary stock market indicators in America, the Standard & Poor's 500, which is most similar to a mutual fund, has an average rate of return of approximately 12% since its inception. Note that this is an average. This means in some individual years people made money and in other years they lost money.

On the other end of the risk spectrum we have our savings account, which has almost no risk of losing money. But, the interest rate you'll earn, or your reward, will be less, say 1%, because of this reduced risk. It's important to note that interest rates at the time I wrote this book are some of the lowest in the history of the United States. With that, however, the last time I checked, 1% is still greater than 0%.

To be honest, it will be difficult to earn 12%, as most of the best investors in the world cannot earn that consistently. It is good to be realistic. In the examples in the next section of this Slice, I will use 6% because I believe it is a realistic return for a mutual fund investment, which has a moderate level of risk. You can use a higher or lower percentage when you are creating your own calculations to help you decide what risk is appropriate for you.

(One quick point of clarification is that you may have noticed for the savings account I used the word *interest*. However, for the S&P 500, or other stocks and mutual funds, for example, I used the word *return*. They are technically different topics; however, for the purposes of this book they can be viewed as similar concepts.)

MANAGING YOUR RISK

In addition to selecting an investment type, there are two other primary ways to manage your risk while investing. We already briefly covered one when you learned what a mutual fund was and how it can *diversify* your investments.

How many shirts do you have? My guess is you have more than one. Are all of your shirts the same or are they different? I'll assume they are different. Green, pink, blue, stripes, solids, polka dots, long-sleeve, short-sleeve, with buttons and without. What if you only had one shirt, a white T-shirt? That probably wouldn't work well for a school dance, a job interview or a really cold day. You bought more than one shirt to reduce the risk of not having the right shirt for each occasion. In other words, you *diversified* your shirt portfolio. Some shirts work for certain occasions, while others do not, but hopefully you have a shirt for every occasion. It's the same with your investment portfolio where some investments make you money and others lose money, but hopefully on average you make money.

No one can pick a good investment every time (just like I cannot pick out the perfect shirt every time). Some investments lose money and other investments make money. I think you would agree you would have a better chance of picking an investment that will make money if you had two choices as opposed to one. What if you had hundreds of choices? You would definitely have a better chance than if you only had one choice, that's for sure. Individual mutual funds, for example, can include hundreds of individual investments (shirts). That's diversification and that is why there is less risk if you diversify your investments.

In addition to buying mutual funds, there are other ways to diversify your investments. Another way is to have a portion of your money in multiple types of investments you learned about: savings account (white T-shirt), certificate of deposit (red T-shirt), bond (blue, striped T-shirt), stock (orange, long-sleeve shirt), and mutual fund (purple, polka dot buttoned shirt). As you know, some of these have lower risk and others have higher risk. If you have a portion of your money in all of them, on average, you will have a moderate level of risk. Here are two examples of diversified investment portfolios and example annual returns:

PORTFOLIO EXAMPLE 1

	MF 1	MF 2	MF 3	MF 4	MF 5	MF 6	**TOTAL**
RETURN	-6%	15%	3%	-4%	7%	-8%	**7%**

PORTFOLIO EXAMPLE 2

	STOCK 1	STOCK 2	MF 1	MF 2	BOND	SAVINGS	**TOTAL**
RETURN	-15%	8%	7%	-2%	3%	1%	**2%**

In the first portfolio, you only have one type of investment, a mutual fund, but you own many different funds to diversify even more than a single mutual fund. In the second portfolio, you diversify by having many different investment types. As you can see, some investments lose money and others make money, but the Total of all investments in each of these portfolios made money. Aren't you glad you didn't put all of your money in Stock 1 of Portfolio Example 2?

The other way to manage your risk while investing is by using your advantage you learned in the 1st Slice: *time*. Some days you pick the perfect shirt to wear and everyone compliments you. Then you wear that shirt again the next month and, unfortunately, it is out of style. You decide to give it one last try the following school year and people love it again. It's the same with investments.

Investments don't make money all the time. Some years they make money and other years they lose money. Over time, however, if you have diversified your investment portfolio, your investments will hopefully make money. To give you an idea how time can make an impact, let's look at an investment in the S&P 500 over the past 20 years:

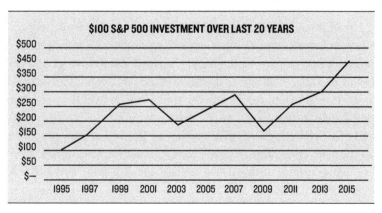

As you can see, if you invested $100 in 1995, you would have turned that $100 into about $450 in 2015. What else do you see? Up and down, up and down, up… In this particular real world example, the increase in investment value around the year 2000 and steep decline subsequent was related to the *dot-com bubble*. The economy recovered over the next years, but around 2008 the *Great Recession* occurred. It is very difficult to guess the exact time an investment will make money.

So, if you know you will need your savings for something else in a year (shorter-term), such as college, then a high-risk investment like a stock may not be a good idea because you might guess the timing wrong. In this case, maybe leaving your money in a lower-risk investment like a certificate of deposit is the best idea. Looking at the chart on the previous page, if you invested your money in 2007 for one year, you would have lost money. But, if you have a long time before you believe you will need those savings, say five years or more (longer-term), then higher-risk investments may make sense for you because you have reduced the risk by using *time* to your advantage; you may have a higher reward with a stock compared to the certificate of deposit. If you invested your money in 2007 and still had that investment today, you would have made money. Your investment would have decreased significantly during this time period, and ups and downs occur with *every* investment you make, but, after time, your investment would have increased in value in this example. Use that *time* advantage of yours and reduce your risk.

The reason I lost my $5,000 in college was because I didn't manage my risk. In fact, I did everything wrong. First, I used my money to buy stocks, the investment type with the highest risk. Then, I only bought one stock at a time; thus, I was not diversified. Lastly, I bought and sold stocks often and did not invest over a long period of time. I didn't know how to manage my risk. Just remember:

LOWER RISK				HIGHER RISK
Diversified	⇨	⇨	⇨	Not Diversified
Long-Term				Short-Term

⑤ Decide what level of risk you're comfortable with. Consider your current financial situation and your goals. Then, determine where you want to invest and open an investment account.

If you are using the *Auto-Saver* tool you learned earlier and you decide the savings account is the right investment type for you, you're done—you're investing! If you decide another type of investment type is what you prefer, you will simply transfer money from your savings account to the other investment type. The next section on compound growth provides you with additional information that might help you make this decision.

COMPOUND GROWTH

> **"The most powerful force in the universe is compound interest."**
>
> —*ALBERT EINSTEIN*

Compound growth is the reason most people invest. Because I know how compound growth works and its benefits, it is one of my best friends when it comes to personal finance. I didn't fully comprehend this concept until I was in my 20s and wish I would have learned it earlier. To this day, this concept gives me motivation to save. It is going to help me retire at the age I want to retire and to reach many other goals along the way. I have a good feeling you and compound growth are going to become really good friends as well after you read this section.

In the previous Investing section, you learned how a 1% annual interest rate turned $1,000 into $1,010 after a year. What if the rate was higher than 1%? I believe 6% is a realistic rate of return for

mutual funds. Earning 6%, as opposed to $1,010, you'll have $1,060, a $60 return ($1,000 × 6%). This free money will come in handy for many reasons; one reason could be to help pay for college, which we look at in the 4th Slice.

Now let's see what happens if you saved for more than a year. Utilizing the concept of *compound*, you'll earn a return in the future on the money you initially deposited with the bank like in the previous example. *In addition*, you'll earn a return on the return you've earned in the past. Put another way, the return *compounds* on itself. This can be a bit confusing. Let's look at *you* to help clarify.

Reading, video games, or sports, in all of these you have been compounding *your knowledge* over the years. Say you are a star basketball player now. Did you start there? First you learned what the game of basketball was. You then built upon that knowledge and learned what a basketball itself was. And then you built upon that knowledge and learned how to dribble, pass, and shoot, etc. Because you continued to build upon your prior knowledge with new knowledge or, rather, you *compounded your knowledge*, you are the basketball star you are today. Nice work.

Now let's walk through a few financial compound growth examples. Continuing with the previous example, how much is your $1,000 deposit worth at the end of year two? You might think it would just earn another $60 of return; it would be worth $1,120 ($1,060 +$60). Sorry, it's worth more! It's worth $1,124. Here is the math that shows where the extra $4 came from (100% investment + 6% return = 106%):

	JANUARY		RETURN		DECEMBER
Year 1	$1,000	x	106%	=	$1,060
Year 2	$1,060	x	106%	=	$1,124

As you can see, the return for Year 2 is now calculated on the higher amount of $1,060 you had at the end of Year 1 as opposed to the original amount of $1,000. Your initial deposit earns $60 every year like in Year 1. However, the return you earned in prior years helps you earn the additional return this year and into the future. In Year 2, the $60 of return you earned in Year 1 earned you the $4 ($60 × 6% = $4). Here's how it looks when you separate out the two components, adding on Year 3 to continue to see how your returns are *working* for you:

YEAR 1			YEAR 2			YEAR 3		
Year 1 Deposit	No Prior Return	Total	Year 1 Deposit	Year 1 Return	Total	Year 1 Deposit	Year 1&2 Return	Total
$1,000	$ -	$1,000	$1,000	$ 60	$1,060	$1,000	$ 124	$1,124
×106%	106%		106%	106%		106%	106%	
=$1,060	$ -	$1,060	$1,060	$ 64	$1,124	$1,060	$ 131	$1,191

For Year 3, we had the $60 of return we earned on our initial deposit in Year 2 *and* we had the $64 of return we earned during Year

1 and Year 2 ($60 in Year 1, which grew by $4 in Year 2 to $64) or $124 ($60 + $64) *working* for us in addition to the initial $1,000. That $1,124 ($1000 + $124) turned into $1,191 by the end of Year 3. That's $191 ($1,191 – $1,000) of free money. Your money is really *working* for you!

And the good news keeps coming. Generally, your returns will compound on a monthly basis as opposed to an annual basis. This means even more money for you. The example we just went through was compounded each year. Keeping with the same example, but instead compounding each month (6% / 12 months = 0.5% per month), here's what the first year would look like:

MONTH	BEGINNING		RETURN		END
1	$1,000	x	100.5%	=	$1,005
2	$1,005	x	100.5%	=	$1,010
3	$1,010	x	100.5%	=	$1,015
4	$1,015	x	100.5%	=	$1,020
5	$1,020	x	100.5%	=	$1,025
6	$1,025	x	100.5%	=	$1,030
7	$1,030	x	100.5%	=	$1,036
8	$1,036	x	100.5%	=	$1,041
9	$1,041	x	100.5%	=	$1,046
10	$1,046	x	100.5%	=	$1,051
11	$1,051	x	100.5%	=	$1,056
12	$1,056	x	100.5%	=	$1,062

As you can see, compound monthly has already given you an extra $2 ($1,062 – $1,060) in the first year when compared to compound annually. Okay, okay, I hear what you're saying: "$2, big deal."

It is a big deal. A really big deal, over time.

TIME

We keep coming back to that advantage of yours: *time.* Continuing with this example, compound monthly, how much would your $1,000 be worth after 30 years? Were you lucky enough to double your money and now have $2,000? Watch your money grow over the 30 years:

YEAR	JANUARY	DECEMBER	YEAR	JANUARY	DECEMBER
1	$1,000	$1,062	16	$2,454	$2,605
2	$1,062	$1,127	17	$2,605	$2,766
3	$1,127	$1,197	18	$2,766	$2,937
4	$1,197	$1,270	19	$2,937	$3,118
5	$1,270	$1,349	20	$3,118	$3,310
6	$1,349	$1,432	21	$3,310	$3,514
7	$1,432	$1,520	22	$3,514	$3,731
8	$1,520	$1,614	23	$3,731	$3,961
9	$1,614	$1,714	24	$3,961	$4,206
10	$1,714	$1,819	25	$4,206	$4,465
11	$1,819	$1,932	26	$4,465	$4,740
12	$1,932	$2,051	27	$4,740	$5,033
13	$2,051	$2,177	28	$5,033	$5,343
14	$2,177	$2,312	29	$5,343	$5,673
15	$2,312	$2,454	30	$5,673	$6,023

Your $1,000 is now worth more than $6,000 (rounded)! Did you see how much return you were earning in those later years? A common mistake made is assuming if you saved for less time, say *half* the time, you would still have *half* the money. Unfortunately, that is not the case and you can see this in the previous table. If you only saved for 15 years, you would not have $3,000 (half of $6,000); rather you would only have $2,454. You are earning return now on the return you earned in the past. If there is less return earned in the past, you will not earn as much return in the future, and that's what makes all the difference. That's why it's so important to start early in life.

And what if you saved more than $1,000? Using the same compound growth concept, if at 20 years old (or earlier!) you started saving $25 per month through age 60 (total savings of $12,000 = $25 × 12 months × 40 years), at a 6%, monthly compound rate, you would have $50,000 at age 60! Now that is motivation to save. The power of compound growth is impressive. This even excites me, and I have been doing this for a long time.

In case you were curious, if you had been successful in investing your $12,000 in higher-risk stocks and earned 12% as opposed to 6% in this example, you would have almost $300,000 as opposed to $50,000. In contrast, using a savings account and earning 1% you would have $15,000. Risk versus reward. But, what's most important to see is in all cases your $12,000 was worth more than $12,000 because you took action and invested, regardless of the level of risk you are comfortable with.

Give this calculation a try on your own. There are two popular options to creating your own compound growth calculation. You can either create the calculations in a spreadsheet or you can use an online compound growth calculator. The calculators on **www.bankrate.com** or **www.investor.gov** will work well if you choose the online approach. If you go to **www.bankrate.com**, here are the inputs for the calculator for our previous example:

TITLE	INPUT
Starting amount	$0
Years to save	40
Rate of return	6%
Additional contributions	$25
Frequency	Per month
Interest	Compound monthly

The result should be approximately $50,000, the same as our example.

❺ Create a compound growth calculation. Decide how much you are going to save, for how long, and with which investment type to estimate your rate.

You may be thinking, "**I'm young and have plenty of time,**" right? Then you may also be thinking, why not have a lot more fun for 20 years by spending that money and only save for 20 years (total savings of $6,000, half of $12,000) and be good with half of the $50,000 or $25,000? This is the common mistake people make (mentioned a few paragraphs prior). Unfortunately, compound growth doesn't work that way. If you only saved for 20 years, you would only have about $11,000 as opposed to $25,000. That's a huge difference! In the previous calculation you can see how the later years made all of the difference and, wow, what a difference they made!

On the flip side, however, what if you saved for 50 years instead of 40 years (total savings of $15,000 = $25 × 12 months × 50 years)? Just 10 more years and $3,000 ($15,000 - $12,000) more savings? Remember the importance of the later years and all of the return you will be earning in those years. You would have close to $100,000. This is double the amount compared to 40 years! I know, $100,000 seems like a huge number, and it is a huge number, but it is very real.

Here is a summary of our examples:

MONTHLY SAVINGS	$25	$25	$25	$25	$0
YEARS SAVING	50	40	39	20	Entire Life
RATE OF RETURN	6%	6%	6%	6%	6%
END SAVINGS	$95,000	$50,000	$47,000	$11,000	$0

Each year you are saving only $300 ($25 × 12 months), but each year you wait to start you are losing thousands of dollars. Take a look at the difference between saving 39 years compared to 40 years. This could be the difference in starting at 16 or 17 years of age. In just one year you lost $3,000 in savings!

It's much easier on yourself to start early and grow your savings in the long run. Ask yourself: "Would I rather spend that $25 each month, or would I rather have money for a car, a home, or $100,000 for retirement and whatever else life brings in between?"

Can you afford *not* to save? You choose.

💲 Once you have an account, find your bank or investment statement. Watch your account grow for a few months because of the amounts you saved and the amounts related to compound growth.

GROWING YOUR SAVINGS SUMMARY

Compound growth—what a beautiful thing. Taking this free money is one of the most common ways people create wealth over time. You just have to decide what the right level of investment risk is for you. It doesn't need to be scary as long as you're comfortable with the risk you're taking and managing it. Some people prefer the higher risk for the potentially higher reward, but others don't. Both are the right answers for each individual.

Until you understand investing as well as you would like, you could stick with the lower-risk investments. As long as you're saving, you're succeeding in getting closer to achieving your goals. Compound growth is an added benefit and I hope you enjoy that benefit someday soon.

REAL WORLD KNOWLEDGE SHARING

- What are five common types of investments?
- What are the risks of investing and how can you manage those risks?
- What is a mutual fund and why is it a good or bad investment?
- What do you like best about compound growth?

BONUS! COMBINING CONCEPTS: BUYING A CAR

Since we like getting crazy, let's combine two of the concepts you have learned: saving and growing your savings. Say you're deciding between two cars and the price difference is $500. You decide the extra $500 is worth it and buy the more expensive car. You could have *saved* the $500, so let's look at it as savings you're *losing*.

Moving onto growing your savings, let's use those new skills of yours and compound the return on that $500. Assume you made this decision at age 20. At age 60, assuming a 6% return, that $500 would have turned into about $5,000. That's the power, good and bad, of compound growth.

When I graduated college I went out and bought a brand-new car. Was that the best financial decision? Probably not. But, I enjoyed that car and I saved money by reducing the amount of money I spent on other things so I could prioritize the new car since it was important to me at the time. Nowadays, a car isn't as important to me. At the time I wrote this book I was driving a car over a decade old with about 180,000 miles on it. Saving, family, friends, and travel are my priorities these days.

Perhaps you still want the more expensive car because it's important to you to have one that is more reliable. For some, memories of driving around in a convertible are priceless. To others, knowing the difference would lead them to choose the less expensive car or to not even buy the car and utilize public transportation such as the local bus. It's just important to know what you're getting into so you can make the right decision for you.

💲 Try combining a calculation for the two concepts, saving and growing your savings. Maybe the cost of college would be a good example to use for this exercise, or the cost of coffees over a lifetime!

NOTES

NOTES

NOTES

4TH SLICE: DEBT

As I said at the beginning of the book, unfortunately you're never too young to do *something* that will negatively impact your finances. That *something* can be a bad decision with debt.

For many, debt has a significant negative impact on their savings because it is generally for more expensive items. Remember when you answered for the question of **"Where did all of my money go?"** Debt would definitely be part of the list, such as a car or student loan. Credit cards are another risky type of debt. You may purchase less expensive items with your credit card, such as clothes or shoes, but after a while they can add up to much larger amounts.

You've worked hard at successfully learning and applying the saving and growing your savings concepts in the previous Slices. Let's add some cheese to our personal finance pizza and learn more about debt to make sure it doesn't get in the way of you and your hard-earned money.

GETTING TO KNOW DEBT

Debt is also known as *credit* or a *loan*. Simply, debt is whenever someone lends you money. For example, the next time you borrow $20 from your friend, you now have *debt*.

There are two primary financial risks associated with debt. The first is you have to *pay* interest on the amount you borrowed. In the 3rd Slice you learned that when you lend banks your money they pay you interest. Debt is where the bank or credit card company is lending you money and, to be fair, you'll have to pay them interest. The interest you have to pay in relation to debt can be significant—we'll calculate interest in an example later in this section.

The second is the risk of overspending. Generally, creditors such as banks and credit card companies will lend you much more than you may be able to afford. This is exciting for people who don't fully understand the risks of debt as they can suddenly buy things they thought they could never afford such as fancy cars and big houses, or many small purchases that add up over time on a credit card. After the excitement of purchasing those items wears off, however, reality sets in that they have to pay back all that money—money they may not have because they are living beyond their means.

DEBT RISKS: *interest* and overspending

Maybe you want a car, but you can't afford one so you decide to get a car loan. Perhaps it is a bunch of smaller purchases, such as music concert or movie tickets you can't afford but want to be with your friends. Or maybe you and your family did not save enough money and are not able to buy groceries or pay rent. These stressful situa-tions can lead to taking on debt you cannot afford. In the short-term, the debt might feel like a good solution; after all, you now have a car like all of your friends. But, if you cannot afford the car, that negative financial decision may stick with you for a very long time.

Overspending and living beyond your means is a bad decision with debt.

However, if you have carefully thought about the item you want to buy with debt and know you can afford it, debt can be a way to achieve your goals such as paying for college or buying a home. Others prefer to be debt free their entire lives, as they don't want to risk overspend-ing and the stress that goes along with it. These individuals save their money over time and only buy items when they have enough money.

If you understand the risks and benefits of debt, you'll see there's no right answer for everyone, but there is a right answer for you. Let's learn more about a few specific types of debt to help you make this decision. One very common form of debt is credit cards. We can start there.

CREDIT CARDS

I have credit cards. But I am careful with them. Credit card debt can get really scary if you overspend.

THE GOOD

Some people don't like carrying cash, whether it's for security or they don't want to have to find an ATM and pay the related fees; thus, the convenience of a credit card is nice.

Also, using a credit card can impact your credit score. Your credit score, which is automatically calculated on your behalf, indicates the likelihood of you repaying your debts. Potential future creditors of yours, such as banks and landlords, will be very interested in this score because it shows them how likely it is that you will pay your bills. If you don't pay off the credit card or pay it late, it hurts your credit score. If you pay off the credit card on time and in full, it helps your credit score. A higher credit score can increase your chances of getting that apartment from the landlord and reducing the interest you have to pay on that debt you may want from a bank someday.

Further, credit card statements list each purchase you made in a month and are easy to review. So, when answering the question of "Where did all of my money go?" from the 2nd Slice, your credit card statement can be helpful in making your list of what you spent your money on. And some credit cards offer rewards for using their cards—for example, free cash back. But that is not always a good thing.

THE BAD

Free cash back sounds good. But did you know credit card companies earn billions of dollars each year? How can they earn that much money if they are giving all of this free cash back to you? Well, free cash back can be good, but this is one marketing technique credit card companies use to get you to overspend. You may get $20 cash back, but you needed to spend a lot of money in order to get it.

For example, for a credit card that gives you 2% cash back on items you purchased, you needed to *spend* $1,000 to *earn* that $20 ($1,000 × 2%). If you were going to spend the $1,000  anyway, then this $20 is truly free money and that's a good thing. However, if you weren't going to spend any of this $1,000, then you actually *lost* $980 ($1,000 − $20). In this case, you've overspent.

This marketing technique of the credit card companies works well, unfortunately. A study by Dun & Bradstreet showed people with credit cards spend 12–18% more on average when compared to people who only use cash. If you're overspending by 15% and earning 2% cash back, you're actually *losing* 13% (15% – 2%).

It's the convenience of a credit card that gets people into trouble. With all of those convenient opportunities to store your credit card information online for quick checkouts, or being able to pay with your phone at stores, these overspending statistics may get worse. It's just psychologically more difficult for people to hand over actual cash than it is to hand over a piece of plastic, click online, or swipe a phone. Paying with a piece of plastic—that's not real money, right? But it is real money, *very* real.

Spending more than you can afford leads to a higher risk of not paying off the credit card in full and on time. And if you don't, you'll have to pay interest to the credit card company. And the interest rate is very, very—let me add another one—*very* high. Some credit cards offer you low *introductory* rates, another marketing technique, but after a short period of time the interest rates increase significantly. Let's go through an example.

A REAL WORLD EXAMPLE

Assume you have a $15,000 credit card balance, also known as *principal*, on a credit card.

THEY HAD
$1,600
of debt before
$15,000
JUST LIKE HIGH
SCHOOL SENIORS

The $15,000 used in this example is real. For households carrying debt, this is the average credit card debt according to the Federal Reserve. This is why it is important to overcome mental blocks such as "**I'm young; I'll do it later**" and "**I don't need it.**" I believe the main reason most people get into trouble with credit cards is because they could not successfully save and grow their savings as discussed in the previous Slices. When they didn't have money to buy something, they used their credit card. Then, when they had credit card debt, they couldn't save, which led to more credit card debt the next time they needed to buy something they didn't have money for. It is a vicious cycle that can last a lifetime. The average debt for a high school senior is $1,600, which is also really high. I am going to use the American average of $15,000 in this example to show you how bad it can get. After all, they had $1,600 of debt at some point on their way to $15,000.

Okay, back to the example. Also assume the credit card has a 16% annual interest rate—I told you it was a high rate. Credit cards allow you to make a *minimum payment* each month. For this example, assume the minimum payment is either 2% of the remaining balance or $15, whichever is higher. With $15,000 of credit card debt, if you were to pay the minimum payment each month, how long do you think it would take you to pay off your balance? A year? A couple of years?

44 frustrating *years*   Forty-four years.

Yes, 44 years. The reason it takes such a long time to pay off your credit card by paying the minimum payment is the minimum payment is set very close to the interest you need to pay each month. As a result, you end up almost only paying interest, and the balance ($15,000 in this example) almost entirely remains and you're getting nowhere each month. Here are the calculations:

At the end of the first month, the credit card company would charge you interest of $200 (16% annual rate / 12 months × $15,000 balance). Your balance is now $15,200 ($15,000 + $200). Then you make the minimum payment, which is $300 (2% × $15,000). Yes, $300—that is a lot of money. As a result, your balance is now $14,900 ($15,200 − $300). As you can see, you only reduced your balance by $100 as the other $200 of your payment only paid off the interest. Here's how the entire first year would look:

MONTHS	BEGIN		INTEREST		MINIMUM PAYMENT		END
1	$ 15,000	+	$ 200	−	$ 300	=	$ 14,900
2	$ 14,900	+	$ 199	−	$ 298	=	$ 14,801
3	$ 14,801	+	$ 197	−	$ 296	=	$ 14,702
4	$ 14,702	+	$ 196	−	$ 294	=	$ 14,604
5	$ 14,604	+	$ 195	−	$ 292	=	$ 14,507
6	$ 14,507	+	$ 193	−	$ 290	=	$ 14,410
7	$ 14,410	+	$ 192	−	$ 288	=	$ 14,314
8	$ 14,314	+	$ 191	−	$ 287	=	$ 14,218
9	$ 14,218	+	$ 190	−	$ 284	=	$ 14,124
10	$ 14,124	+	$ 188	−	$ 283	=	$ 14,029
11	$ 14,029	+	$ 187	−	$ 280	=	$ 13,936
12	$ 13,936	+	$ 186	−	$ 279	=	$ 13,843
Total			$ 2,314		$ 3,471		

At the end of the first year you've paid $3,471 in minimum payments, but unfortunately you've only reduced your balance by $1,157 ($15,000 – $13,843). The other $2,314 only paid for interest. Let's look at the entire 44 years it would take you to pay off your balance (table shows total amount paid during the period of years; for example, 1–10 is for the first 10 years in total):

YEARS	BEGIN		INTEREST		MINIMUM PAYMENTS		END
1-10	$15,000	+	$16,556	-	$24,834	=	$6,722
11-20	$6,722	+	$7,459	-	$11,189	=	$2,992
21-30	$2,992	+	$3,320	-	$4,981	=	$1,331
31-40	$1,331	+	$1,469	-	$2,273	=	$527
41-44	$527	+	$189	-	$716	=	$0
Total			$28,994		$43,994		

As you can see, not only would it take you 44 frustrating years of payments to pay off your $15,000 balance, but also you'll pay an additional $28,994 in interest over that time for a total of $43,994. That is a lot of money.

To calculate the above on your own, you can use a spreadsheet program or you can use an online credit card calculator such as the one at **www.bankrate.com**.

❺ By using a spreadsheet program or online calculator, calculate a credit card repayment schedule. How much interest would you have to pay and how long would it take you to pay off the balance?

SOME HELP

What's the silver lining in all of this? That you now have this knowledge, and knowledge is power.

If you currently have credit card debt, don't panic; it is what it is and you can only work on a solution. One potential solution is to pay more than the minimum payment each month. That way you'll be paying off more of the balance as opposed to only the interest. In the previous example, if you were to pay a fixed amount of $300 per month (as opposed to the potential minimum of $15) you would pay off your balance in seven years as opposed to 44 years. Also, you'd pay interest of about $10,000 or total payments of about $25,000 ($15,000 balance + $10,000 in interest) as opposed to the almost $44,000 in the previous example. That $300 a month is a lot of money, but cutting off 37 years and $19,000 of interest payments is huge.

Also, some credit card companies will reduce the interest rate if you just ask them to. All it takes is a phone call, and the worst they can say is no; it is worth your time to give it a try. In any event, the goal is to get out of credit card debt as soon as you can so you can get back to saving.

⑨ If you have credit card problems right now, don't panic. Take what you've learned, come up with a plan to get out of credit card debt, and stick with that plan no matter what.

If you are not currently in credit card debt, perhaps this is motivation to save $25 a month like the example in the 2nd Slice of this book and stay out of a credit card mess altogether.

If you believe you need a credit card, there are a few cards out there that offer cash back when you purchase something and, in addition, when you pay the credit card bill. This may be a nice option as it may incentivize you to pay *is this motivation to save?* your bill. Also, some credit cards try to charge people annual fees, so potentially avoid these credit cards.

In addition, there are tricks you can use to help stop credit card issues. One trick is to set your credit card *spending limit* very low, maybe $500, or as low as you can. A *spending limit* is the maximum balance you can charge to your credit card. If you attempt to charge a purchase that puts you over this limit in total, your card will be rejected and you will not be able to make the purchase, which, in this case, is a good thing. This means the maximum balance you could have is $500. The credit card companies often offer you a very high spending limit, say $10,000. Some people believe qualifying for a high spending limit is a good thing, but for most it is not. Your risk of overspending would be greatly decreased if your spending limit was only $500 as opposed to $10,000. To reduce your spending limit, just call your credit card company or go online to their website and make this request.

When I graduated high school and was off to college, my mom got me a credit card through our local credit union. She wanted me to have it in case of an emergency and to help establish my credit score, with one non-negotiable point: a $500 spending limit. I still thank her to this day. My mom worked at the credit union, and I was lucky to have such a good teacher.

⊗ **If you have a credit card, contact your credit card company and learn what your spending limit is. Decrease the spending limit as much as you can as soon as you can.**

If you get a credit card, pay it back, in full and on time. This is how I am careful with credit cards. I can't stress the importance of this enough in your journey toward personal finance success because of the issues illustrated in the previous examples.

DEBIT CARDS

A *credit* card is not the only type of plastic card available to you. A *debit* card is a great alternative. As you learned above, a credit card is a form of debt, as the credit card company is loaning you money or, put another way, is extending you credit for your purchases. A debit card, however, is not debt at all. Rather, it is another form of cash, your own cash. The debit card is linked to your bank account, and when you make a purchase it takes money directly out of your account. You can use a debit card for purchases at your neighborhood store, online, and almost all other places credit cards are accepted. And, since you are not borrowing any money from anyone when using a debit card, you don't have to pay any interest like you do with a credit card. As you already know, interest can be expensive.

With a debit card you do still have the risk of overspending, as it is still easy enough to hand over that piece of plastic. However, you will only be able to spend what you have in your bank account. This significantly reduces your risk of overspending compared to a credit card, because with a credit card, as you know, you can spend up to your spending limit, which may be money you don't actually have.

Another common way people use debit cards is to withdraw cash from an ATM. This way they are using cash and reducing their risk of overspending as well. Also, similar to the trick of setting your spending limit low on a credit card to reduce your risk, you can do something similar with a debit card. With a debit card you can set a maximum daily purchase limit and, in addition, a maximum limit of how much cash you can withdraw from an ATM. This can help reduce your risk of overspending too—set those maximums as low as you can.

Those are the primary benefits, risks, and alternatives of credit card debt. Another type of debt you might soon be looking into is a student loan for college. Why don't we learn more about those now.

PAYING FOR COLLEGE

Deciding whether to go to college or not is a big decision. Some will decide not to go to college, as they would rather start working full-time after high school. Others may want to become an entrepreneur and start a business. The right answer to this question is different for everyone.

If you decide to go to college, you will find that there are a lot of colleges out there, and similar to every other purchase you make, that college is a financial decision. Also, similar to all other purchases, you'll have to prioritize. Some students will choose a less expensive *there are* **many ways** *to pay for* **college** college, while others prioritize a more expensive school. I am well aware of the increases in the price of college over recent years; I can understand if this is causing you stress. College is another form of investment. It is an investment in yourself. If college is a goal of yours, I want to share with you a few options to pay for college.

You probably already know the definition of a *scholarship*, but if you don't, a scholarship is free money for college that's awarded to people just like yourself every year. Generally, all you have to do is fill out an application to be eligible for the scholarship.

You can be eligible to receive scholarships for many different reasons. There are scholarships available in relation to academics, athletics, demographics, area of study, and the list goes on. Ask around; a school guidance counselor is a great place to start. You can also research online, for example at **studentaid.ed.gov**, and ask friends and family. Many scholarships go unclaimed each year!

I discussed scholarships with my guidance counselor at school and they helped me apply. I was able to earn a few thousand dollars in scholarships, which really helped out when paying for college. To be honest, I probably could have done more and I wish I would have researched to know all of the scholarships available to me. Find these scholarships, apply, and take advantage of them.

After you've exhausted your scholarship efforts, you may still require financial aid from the government. Not all financial aid needs to be repaid, however. For example, Pell grants are awarded to those with lower household incomes and have a larger financial need. There is not a specific application for Pell; rather, your eligibility for Pell is considered when you apply for general financial aid. If you apply for financial aid you are not required to use it; it might be worth it to you to apply to see if you are eligible for a Pell grant. Another financial aid option that is not a loan is the Federal Work-Study Program. As the name implies, it is a program that provides paid part-time jobs to students with larger financial needs. And, of course, you have worked hard saving, or will be soon after you are done reading this book. You can use that money to help pay for college!

After using these payment options, you may still require financial aid loans. I had to take out student loans, but I thought my college education was worth the investment. Most student loans are from the United States government, and you can defer payment on them until after you leave the college. You then have a fair number of years, generally about 10 years, to pay back the loans. It's important to understand, however, you are required to pay back the loans whether you graduate college or not. Also, note that student loans may or may not cover all of your college costs and, if not, you may need to pay for these excess costs on your own. You can learn more about financial aid at **studentaid.ed.gov** as well.

Similar to all other types of loans, you'll have to pay interest. Student loans generally have a lower interest rate than credit cards, however. For example, if you borrowed $30,000 in student loans, the average student loan debt in America according to The Institute for College Access and Success, at a 5% annual interest rate and paid back the loans over 10 years, you would end up paying a total of about $38,000. As such, you would pay about $8,000 of interest ($38,000 – $30,000).

There are a few tools you can use to help you complete this calculation easily on your own. The first way is to use a loan amortization template. If you are using Excel or a similar spreadsheet program such as Google Sheets, this is a standard worksheet template. In the template you will fill in a few cells, like this:

DESCRIPTION	VALUE
Loan amount	$30,000
Interest rate	5%
Number of years	10 years
Payments each year	12 (1 payment each month)

After you input this information, the template calculates the result automatically for you ($38,000 in this example). It will also calculate the monthly payments for you, which in this case is about $300. It is definitely better to know this information before you agree to the debt.

If you do not have access to a spreadsheet program, another option is to go to the bank you have your bank accounts with and ask them to help you. There are also online *loan amortization* calculators on sites such as **www.bankrate.com**. This specific example is for student loans. However, if you are curious about other types of debt, such as car and home loans, these tools work as well, as the calculation is the same.

⑤ By using a spreadsheet template, asking your bank, or using an online calculator, complete a loan amortization calculation to determine the total amount and your monthly payment on student loans you might be thinking about (or any other type of loan).

DEBT SUMMARY

All types of debt have the risk of overspending and interest payments that can definitely get in the way of you achieving your goals. Before taking on any debt, I always ask myself, "Will I be able to pay back this debt in full and on time?" If the answer is "no" to this question, my answer to the debt is also "no."

To answer this question, go back to the list you made when you were answering the question of "Where did all of my money go?" in the 2nd Slice. Add your potential debt to the list and see if you have enough money for it. If the answer is yes, then debt could be a financial tool for you. *pay back* **IN FULL** *and on time* If the answer is no, then debt may not be for you right now as it could get you into financial trouble.

Many people believe excessive debt was the cause of the latest recession. Since people could not pay back their debts, they had to decrease their everyday spending and, in turn, the economy recessed. This led to high levels of unemployment, significant investment losses, home foreclosures, and many other negative impacts. My guess is you and your family felt the negative impacts of the recession in some way. I sincerely hope you are able to avoid the same mistakes others have made with debt now that you know how it works and its risks.

REAL WORLD KNOWLEDGE SHARING

- What are the two primary risks with any debt?
- What are the best ways to protect yourself against credit card debt?
- How is a debit card different than a credit card?
- How do you know if you can afford debt?
- What are the different ways you can pay for college?

NOTES

NOTES

NOTES

NOTES

THE END

You now have the crust, sauce, and cheese of your personal finance pizza. I truly hope you enjoyed reading this book. First and foremost, I hope this book helped you overcome your mental block toward personal finance so you can continue to build the confidence that you can be successful—because you can.

It's now time for you to take action. Here's a summary of the to-do items listed throughout the book:

THE SHORTER LIST

- Overcome your mental block.
- Save.
- Don't get into trouble with debt or investing.

THE LONGER LIST

INTRODUCTION

- Think about and determine your mental block. Keep it in mind as you read this book to help you overcome. This will be the most important thing you do if you want to be successful in personal finance.

1st SLICE: YOU

YOUR GOALS

- Think about your goals and write them down. Have fun with this one; it's your chance to dream big. For this and all other exercises in this book I have created templates for you to fill in if you like. You can find them at **www.overcomepublishing.com/solution/**.

YOUR PRIORITIZATION

- Think about what's important to you. How will you prioritize your spending to help achieve your goals?

2nd SLICE: SAVING

HOW DO I SAVE?

- Create two accounts at your bank and set up the automatic transfer to Auto-Save.

WHERE DID ALL OF MY MONEY GO?

- Keep track of everything you spend next week or month using a spreadsheet or any other format that works best for you. Are any changes necessary to reach your goals? Prioritize, prioritize, prioritize.

Ⓢ   Make a list of all of the *small stuff* in your life that you can live without if it meant helping you reach your goals.

3RD SLICE: GROWING YOUR SAVINGS

INVESTING

Ⓢ Decide what level of risk you're comfortable with. Consider your current financial situation and your goals. Then, determine where you want to invest and open an investment account.

COMPOUND GROWTH

Ⓢ Create a compound growth calculation. Decide how much you are going to save, for how long, and with which investment type to estimate your rate.

Ⓢ Once you have an account, find your bank or investment account statement. Watch your account grow for a few months because of the amounts you saved and the amounts related to compound growth.

Ⓢ Try combining a calculation for the two concepts, saving and growing your savings. Maybe the cost of college would be a good example to use for this exercise, or the cost of coffees over a lifetime!

4TH SLICE: DEBT

CREDIT CARDS

Ⓢ By using a spreadsheet program or online calculator, calculate a credit card repayment schedule. How much interest would you have to pay and how long would it take you to pay off the balance?

Ⓢ If you have credit card problems right now, don't panic. Take what you've learned, come up with a plan to get out of credit card debt, and stick with that plan no matter what.

Ⓢ If you have a credit card, contact your credit card company and learn what your spending limit is. Decrease the spending limit as much as you can as soon as you can.

PAYING FOR COLLEGE

Ⓢ By using a spreadsheet template, asking your bank, or using an online calculator, complete a loan amortization calculation to determine the total amount and your monthly payment on student loans you might be thinking about (or any other type of loan).

And I am going to add one last item to the list: Don't give up, ever. What will your to-do list be?

Go at your own pace so you're not over-whelmed. You can start with only one item from the list above, perfect it, and then move on to the next. Or, perhaps you are eager and want to get going on a few of them at once.

Don't **EVER** *give up!*

You don't want to get too full of pizza and never want to eat it again (okay, maybe that isn't possible), if you know what I mean. If you're saving, you're succeeding.

Most people just starting out with personal finance will make a mistake, as you know I did. What's important is learning from your mistake, continuing to be successful with personal finance, and achiev-

mistakes **are OK!**

ing your goals. When you are able to pay for that wedding or car, it will all be worth it. And when you think it's appropriate in the future, perhaps a year from now, check and see how you're doing on your financial goals. No one gets it right the first time.

Use my Facebook page *(I Want More Pizza Book)* as often as you can. Sharing real life experiences, positive and negative, we can learn from will be very powerful for you and for others. You could also create a personal finance club at school with your friends and classmates. Your family might want to get involved too. They may be able to help you, and my guess is you will be able to help them as well.

In closing, I just want to acknowledge the courage it took for you to read this book and the courage you will demonstrate when you apply these concepts in your real life and share them with others. You may not believe it, but I'm certain you're now far ahead of many people with respect to personal finance. Many believe someone else will help them out or money works its way out on its own, but, unfortunately, you now know that's not the case. With that, you're a long way toward being a happier and healthier person.

The next time you're out to dinner with friends and family, take a moment and sit back and smile—you've taken control of your financial future and they are proud of you for it. Oh, and have a slice of pizza for me.

Oh, sorry….The End.

(Or, rather, the beginning of your financial success.)

TOPPINGS?

If you just can't get enough, below are a few more topics you can research to add some toppings to your personal finance pizza, or you can ask me on my Facebook page (*I Want More Pizza* Book) about them and I'll be glad to help you learn. As you can see, they all lead back to *savings*.

as long as you're *saving,* you're succeeding

- **TAXES** — Similar to the *sales tax* that is added to the receipt when you buy your favorite shoes, there's a similar *income tax* that reduces your paycheck. You have to pay taxes, but there are ways to pay fewer taxes and, in turn, have more savings.

- **RETIREMENT** — It will come someday and most aren't ready, as they don't have enough savings. Start with the topic of Individual Retirement Arrangements (IRAs) or a 401(k) program.

- **INFLATION** — Your favorite candy bar cost $0.75 a few years ago and now it costs $1...ugh. The price increase is an example of inflation and most likely will never stop. Yet another good reason to save.

- **INSURANCE** — From car insurance to health insurance, this is a way to protect your savings. Lack of sufficient health insurance is the number one cause of bankruptcy in America according to NerdWallet and Debt.org (followed by job loss and credit debt).

- **IDENTITY THEFT** — Having your identity stolen can significantly harm your savings and, in turn, your financial future.

NOTES

NOTES

NOTES

NOTES

ABOUT THE AUTHOR

My name is Steve Burkholder and I had the same questions as you about personal finance at one point or another in my life. Everyone does.

In high school, I mowed lawns and had a part-time job at McDonald's. I had a paycheck in my hand and thought the sky was the limit. Then, surprises, emergencies, and the real world arrived. I was lucky enough to have family that understood personal finance and was willing to teach it to me. I am forever thankful.

I graduated from the University of Minnesota Carlson School of Management; focusing in the areas of finance and accounting. After university, I worked as a CPA for one of the largest public accounting firms in the world in multiple states and internationally. I'm now a member of a Corporate Finance department at a higher education institution. I have a wife and daughter and we love to travel and experience various cultures every chance we get.

I personally use every single concept in *I Want More Pizza* and really enjoy teaching them to others. If you're curious as to what my favorite concept is, it's the Auto-Saver (although, compound growth is a close second). It's so simple, yet so effective. As a third generation educator, helping others learn is what our family has a passion for. Volunteering with Junior Achievement educating students about personal finance is what motivated me to create this resource. I now spend my educational time teaching the concepts in this book to middle and high school students.

While my name is on the book as the author, I definitely cannot take all of the credit. It took about 65 talented individuals to create this book including other finance professionals, middle and high school teachers and students, publishing professionals, and, of course, educational expertise from my family.

ABOUT THE AUTHOR (CONTINUED)

I hope this book provides you with answers to many of your questions and helps you achieve all of your life goals that support your values, including giving back to the community. Some of us have family, friends, or others to help us with this important topic; others don't. As you learn, please pass your knowledge along to another. Together, what a difference we'll make.

Thank you for for having the courage to read and apply the concepts in this book in your life. I wish you all the best.

CPSIA information can be obtained
at www.ICGtesting.com
Printed in the USA
LVHW04s2333290518
578955LV00009B/210/P

9 780996 519403